William Holden

I want to die just
Like William Holden did

I want to get drunk and
Fall so that my temple hits
Perfectly on the corner of the coffee table

I want the blood of my
Wretched life to saturate
The lush carpeting, then let
It dry into a scab around by carcass

I want that same shell
To lie undiscovered for days
Til the unbearable summer heat
Creates such a putrid stench
That even the fuckin' flies won't come in

39

This poem would have to be a masterpiece
To capture a spirit like the one in you
It would have to be charming
Beautiful and elegant too
To say what needs to be said about you

No great painter, alive or dead
Could paint the beauty you show to me
A camera could show what's real
By what its lens might see
I think any photographer would agree

No musician, no matter how great
Or how hard he tried to put you in the song
Couldn't make his music with your charisma
The most exquisite note would still be wrong
Your voice alone sings the greatest song

No work of art would ever do you justice
Your soul is elusive and engaging
Taxing an artist, convoluting the image
And still the creativity is raging

Throngs walked past me
Sudden horror in their eyes
One eye bloodied shut
The other on their thighs

Scanning the crowd
Beneath a leaking head
Won't one of you sluts
Share the comfort of my bed

Pledging on my child's grave
To shower jelly from my face
Suck my fucking dick
Just rid me of disgrace

Stagger to the car
Offers of help seem to abound
It's a minor situation
Like screams without a sound

Right in the rearview mirror
Is the damage that's been done
Tons of caked on blood
Oh Lord, isn't this fun

40

Sometimes it seems like
I'm just walking in the night
Then I'm in a hallway
But at least it has a light

The hall is long and curved
Its path goes every which way
Hundreds of doors on either side
Millions of rules to obey

Every door that I open
Comes at some kind of cost
Some doors offer satisfaction
Other doors leave me hopelessly lost

Once in a while
The hallway has a window
So I look outside
Is there somewhere I should go?

Now, when I see a door
I wonder if I should knock
Whenever I'm not wanted
I wished it had a lock

I'm drawn to certain doors
I want it with a taste
I usually don't have the key
Somehow it go misplaced

Should I, or shouldn't I go in
I need to stop running and take a stance
Then a long door opens
And I know I have to take the chance

231

I'm human
I don't really care
No matter
What happens to you
If you get sick
Or if you die
I'm still going to
Have to wake up for
Work tomorrow
And you will be in the hospital
Or the cemetery
The sun will keep
Coming up
And it will keep
Going down

You're a light upon the darkness street
You are the diamonds in my eyes
Every time you're around, I feel hypnotized
Please let me tell you how I feel
And show you how I care
You're all I want and all I think
I know that you are aware
Since I met you a while ago
Things haven't been the same
There's a new voice in my heart
All it does is call your name

So many people standing
At the bus stop and
Spend their whole
Life waiting for
A bus that
Will
Never
Ever
Come

Oh little girl
Why must you pass my eyes
If you can never be
More than a temptation on my soul
Oh God in heaven
Why do you test me this way
A beauty, barely half my age
Prancing and skipping all over
This scarred heart of mine
Oh Father Time
Must the clock keep ticking
Please freeze it all so I can
Study this living, breathing art wok
Oh little girl
Do you tease when I'm so low
Look at my badge of loneliness
Show me some mercy
If you're going to leave so soon
Next time don't come at all

I'm not dead yet
But flies landing on me
I don't brush them away
I don't try to kill them
I just watch them
Are they laying eggs on me?
Taking in maggots through osmosis
I can already feel them
Gnawing their way inside out
Nobody would ever know
And even fewer would be surprised
To them I have already rotted
The maggots are simply a cleanup crew
How long?
How long before the shell cracks?
How long before I'm seen?
I eat healthy
And swallow vitamins daily
It makes the maggots stronger
And they eat through the shell
Exposing a barely beating heart
A fly lands on it
I worry about its offspring

141

Give me just a
Little time with
My daughter
Make me feel human
Once again
So I fell like
I'm not a slave
To the system that
Fills me with hate
Clear and concise
But she fills me
With love
Like watching a
Cloudy pink sunrise
Or getting a massage

Yeah, you're right, it's rainin'
And as usual, you're depressed
You've been doing drugs all night
Don't you think you need some rest

It's so great to be an artist
And justify yourself that way
The Space Needle isn't literal

This ain't fuckin' Seattle

FOR EMILY

It was then, I walked in from the cold
No feeling, no direction, no emotion
Like a dinghy anchored in the thundering surf
Merely serving its purpose in the eternal ocean

With the bitter chill barely gone away
Human silhouettes passing before my eyes
A refreshing and familiar face danced by
The summer sun pierced the winter night skies

Silently, and desperately in awe
Every cell in my body was excitedly alive
My heart pounded harder with each step you neared
Get hungrier and hungrier for you to arrive

Meeting with a hug that shocked my senses
A feeling of joy that I've been missing for so long
Resurgence in the greatness of life
A giant tide flowing ever so strong

Those moments are too few, too far between
I can't complain, I do the best I can
If I had died at that very moment
I assure you, I'd have died a happy man

Sometimes I feel so far gone
Then I realize I am still here
The light is so damn bright
I know the darkness is near
Always the sun rises
The sky turns orange and black
I think I'm being followed
Too much of a man to look back
Paranoid
      Hungry
           Swallowing hard
Can't catch my breath
Sweat drips from my face
I can think only about life and death
Born in a gunshot
Squeezed by a cold hard hand
Missing all the targets
Simply can't meet demand
Bullet keeps moving
Forever is never the ride
You wake up one morning
Realizing you are already dead

127

A snowy Tuesday morning
This is so nice
It's 9:30 a.m.
Been to the liquor store twice

Saw the sky outside
Didn't want to go to work today
I used to be functional
But it's all slipping away

Everything is so bleak
It stopped snowing too soon
A few more beers
I'll be passed out by noon

Smooth called
Right around four
Had to compare notes
Who'd been drinking more

Then we promised
We'd touch base at eight
Just to see who was in
The most drunken state

132

It's hard for me not to smile
When I'm inside of you
It's hard for me not to cry
I've loved all you women
But I've watched so many of you die

I've floated down the river of your blood
And roasted in the sun of your eyes
I've understood your many truths
And realized most of your lies

Whatever happened between us
I guess we went separate ways
I always feel like part of you
Most of my friends have left
But nearly everybody stays

You dance wildly across the desert
Your extremities are so extreme
A lively tango with the past
I've waltzed into today
The present isn't what it might seem

So here I am as an outsider
Even on the inside I'm looking in
It's been a long damn time
But show me some forgiveness
You have no idea where I've been

Your sunsets are so brilliant
You can melt me with your charm
Your depressions came close to breaking me
I packed my bags for far away
How come you never protected me from harm?

I still watch your body longingly
Believe me when I say that I'm loyal
I will always be in love with you
But I keep trying to walk away
Even when I've left so many buried in your soil

34

Nobody had seen his face before
That day at the bar and grill
Whether others come to eat and drink
The stranger came to kill
The owner, Roger, was at the bar
Asked the man what was his choice
"This won't take long," he said
In a Charles Bronson Voice
He slipped the machine gun
Out from under his coat
Before a word was said
The stranger shot Roger in the throat
People screamed and ducked below
As bullets sprayed all around
The stranger laughed and laughed
As sixteen bodies hit the ground
He dropped the gun to his side
Then held it high instead
Suddenly his smile disappeared as he put the gun to
his own head
One last shot was heard
It echoed through the sky
The faceless, nameless stranger
Never told a single soul why

The Twelve Disciples

Call in the marketing team
How should we make it seem?
They say that there are angels there
Put that in the graphics department's care
Goddammit, tell the cameraman
To get the bullet scars square

Make sure the interview
Focuses on seeing Jesus that day
Then they'll believe
And then they'll pay
We'll rearrange the edits
We'll make a thousand 4-20-99 Tuesdays

Disciples are the new names for victims
We need dollars to make it work
The choice is yours
This is the son of Pat Robertson
Signing off for the
Christian Broadcasting Network

Where do your thoughts wander
What visions race through your brain
Have I ever crossed your mind
Is my attraction to you in vain
Maybe loneliness has me reaching afar
Can you see the corner of my eye watching you
Aren't we both traveling the same road
Do you want the same thing
Or something new
Is our passing nothing but coincidence
Do I wish it to be some kind of fate
Do I wish for the possibility that it isn't going to
happen
Would patience be easier if there was no wait
Are you just beauty that I may never know
What is the mystery I see in your eyes?
Can your hair be as soft as it looks
How do you separate reality from lies?
Is it all right to hope for more than a glance
Will you let me dream that there is no chance

35

Oh what tricks the mind can play
If you let your weapon wander away
Wild thought waves dance in the night
Crumbling the edges of dark and light
You close your eyes and only see red
Now your mind controls your head
What a shock your brain has been left behind
Why is reality always so hard to find?

5

The room is dark
I see your silhouette
It gets me excited
The closer that you get
Your scent is already here
Oh, that sweet perfume
Your mere presence
Illuminates the room
Slowly you walk over
Your touch
Well aware, I can tell
Never too much
A kiss and a lick
What a glorious taste
I'm gonna eat you
The face to the feet

239

Ten straight hours of cocaine
Just got in a head on collision
The seal was tongued until clean
Here is the hell I hate to envision

Four a.m. watching a video
Too damn wired to pay attention
Even Jack Nicholson can't hold me
Hornier than I care to mention

Wish I could have run out earlier
Lonely so I guess I'll masturbate
Pornographic pictures in my brain
Cumming all over my imaginary mate

As the last bit drains to the curls
I'm content again to be alone
No worries about her orgasm
Nothing more to do except watch the phone

223

It's been so hot lately
The car won't run most times
Clouds are rollin' through
And they will bring the rains
Rinsing blood from the sidewalk
Born out of last night's heat
Thankful I wasn't there
That taste is already gone
I'm satisfied by the refrigeration
That is pumped through the aorta
All of a sudden I'm on my knees
Praying to the good lord above
Not really that bad of a guy
Guess the rain won't come after all
Not much blood on the concrete
Sooner or later it'll go away

224

A quick stroke for Mary
At my defense
When things got scary
For the complaints I've generated
And to all of the anger
You've allowed to be venerated
I feel something should
Be said for her
Who has the most shit to endure?
And for those I left seething
Like a baby who was teething
I raise up a toast
And offer some good cheers
For the woman that
Must deal with all of the women
That I've left in tears
And I hope it will derail
Some of the messages
You hear on your voice mail

ZOMBIE TANGO

Time left them dull
The rough edges of youth
Had been smoothed away

Their eyes no longer
Held the glare of fight
The ambitions they held
Were forgotten for routine

It had been five years
We knew the change would come
We were anxious to see how
Those dreams were progressing

Some gained an inch
Others a mile
Most of the dreams
Had vanished altogether

Some had new dreams
To help them forget
They had nothing in the past
It promised a better future

So those dead dreams
Join those that never existed
Now they dance the zombie tango

WHAT YOU SEE

You'll never do the things
That you doubt you can achieve
Things would turn out differently
If only you'd believe

The power of the mind
Is usually the answer
Negativity, all too often
Grows and spreads like cancer

Advice is nice
But it's really up to you
If you win or lose
When all of the playing is through

If you don't see yourself somewhere
That's a place you'll never be
Even in total darkness
A believer can still see

I'm just talking
Not trying to preach
But how high you get
Depends on how high you reach

142

For some sick
Reason I fell
Your pain
I saw him
Die
The truck
Rolled over
His chest
And he died
Then he talked
About how
Cold he was
And
Then there was
Nothing left to be done
He just died

29

Cap that mother fucker
Let his blood splatter all over me
I've got nothing to live for
And neither did he
One bullet in the brain
Let's celebrate Halloween
He didn't do anything to me
I just felt a little mean
You're just the same as me
It's a damn fine day to die
Do you think you're leaving here alive?
Hey fuckhead, neither do I
I will pull this trigger
Without a second thought
Look at your blood on the sidewalk
That's the only thing you got
If you want some revenge
I'll spend my life in a cell
But don't worry
We won't need introductions in hell

123

I know a friend
She thinks she's dating a producer
Somebody is slowly realizing
Which one is the loser

31

I can't tell you
What you must learn on your own
Or explain the feeling
When you wake up in a place where you're all alone
Nor will I say
It's a cold world out there and nothing more
That's what I was told
So many years before
At your age
Finding out what life is about
Home is like a prison
An exotic place is your only way out
Your head is filled
Thoughts of riches, truth, and love
Consider yourself lucky
If you find one of the above
It's a crazy fuckin' world
Nothing is ever what it seems
Only inside of yourself can you live your dreams
Go if you must
Find a place where you are free
Don't forget
This is home, it always will be
That doesn't mean much now
It feels good out on the road
Gets pretty damn lonely
A heavy load
The people at home
It can keep you going out there
I won't keep you
It's your turn to find out what's fair
One thing I hope you see
New York, San Diego or Rome
It's a good feeling
To be going home

A MUDDY FIELD

Five strands of barbed wire All directions and one extra

Should I see what

The hell is under

That coffin shaped board

Push the fence down

Climb over it

And see for your fucking self

But why

There's nothing there

Why's the board any different

I know that all it is

Is pipes and veins

With tons and tons

Of shit

Human shit

Going into the ocean

TWO DAUGHTERS AND A GRAVEYARD GHOST

Theirs was a house of shadows
Mine was a black marble crypt
We mingled as souls in a cemetery
Broken promises made me feel gypped

Those two daughters entranced me
They couldn't leave the demon alone
One at a time I lusted out loud
Dear God, if only I had known

A beauty in the eldest captivated
Tongues of flame in a darkened life
Our eyes were joined in temptation
A longing not to be severed by knife

The younger was alluring
Not to say not lovely as well
Hers was a cerebral seduction
In her own prison, in her own cell

Another cold and moonless night
We had formed a circle of three
They had no fear of my haunting
It binds the union with me

Choruses of gremlins caroused about
It was like a circus atmosphere
Figures fogged by clouds of smoke
I wasn't the only spirit there

The angels never did come
Guess they weren't invited
A destiny just out of reach
Despite the passions they ignited

Waves are crashing on the mausoleum
Bleeding in from the coast
Ours is a story of survival
Two daughters and a graveyard ghost

241

The old man is crawling
Dawn has broken
It's time to leave the sewer
To go scour the gutter
Knows what he's looking for
There's the newsstand
The Wall street Journal
A copy of Barron's Weekly
The old man scurries
He goes back to his hole
And studies his investment options

136

There's nothing to
Masturbate about
In this world
I fondle myself
Constantly
I do get hard
Let me fuck you
Into the
Next century
I
VVill
Do
Anything sexually
That
You
Want
Me
To
Do

47

I hate when you beg
At me
Don't you fucking remember
I'm the one
Who wants to spit in your
Fucking face
Every goddamn time you ask
For a quarter
I swear I had some compassion
At first
I'm only a paycheck away
From you

138

A beautiful woman
With that
She might be
a lesbian
look
and she stared me down
then I called
her bluff
now I'm just
lying around
sucking down beers
and wondering
when would be the
perfect time
to slash my wrists

139

I'm always looking to
Find the influence that you
Play in my life
Which is why

So often find
Recluse
And loneliness
Hanging like a soggy
Grey day over
My life
I love the sun

140

Life, Love and
Mind altering substances
The beginning
The end
All of life's little dances
Mentality
Disguised by lust
A hard on
Faked passion
My dictionary has no trust
Nothing's simple
Seems so hard for me
I whine
But I'm fine
I'm just not who I want to be

130

Goodnight Avenue
City Park Zoo
Childhood dreams
Too far, it seems
Pueblo Reservoir
The girl next door
Watching the river flow
Not feeling myself grow
Pitts Middle School
When I felt like a fool
Motorcycling the hills
Chasing down youthful thrills

46

The only thing

That seems to

 Be missing from

 My life is an

Ankle length

 Black leather

 trench coat

50

At some point in our talks
She told me that she
Had lived in apartments
For her entire life
She didn't mean to
Be a whore but
That's just the way
The little bitch turned out
Taking drugs and beating her kids
Then blaming it all
On loneliness

143

I see the corner of
Your eyes and I see
How they looked at me
You hate me
You want me to die
And I laugh
At the thought
But I'm right here
Not in an asylum
I work
I rent
And I know its
Going to happen
In a frenzied pace
In a frenzied place

1

Sleepwalking
No place in the night
Trash talking
Can't get it right
Fire breathing
There is no peace
Pain writhing
Darkness is my fleece
Thrill seeking
Hello big goodbye
A time to cry

138

Guess I slept a bit
Pretty sure the clock said ten
Something's wrong with me
I'm having that feeling again

Did I misspell that last word?
Because in some way
An alcoholic's poem
Must be absurd

And then comes midnight
Haven't had anything to eat
I look through the cabinets
But there isn't anything sweet

Consciousness lapses, shivering
That was right around two
Nothing to comfort me

But the fridge with one brew

I know that its daybreak
It's just past five
The ink on this paper
Says I'm still alive

134

I keep watching
"Apocalypse Now"
over and
Fucking over again
But
Only the parts
That Bobby Duvall
Is in
Especially
About loving
Napalm
In the morning
I love it
I really fucking do
Don't flinch
Even if it is special effects
Surf
Or
Fight
Make it smell like victory

DOCTOR

The doctor carefully lifts a vial of the deadly substance
His concentration is total
The crimson liquid doesn't look so dangerous
He fears his elbow will bump the sink
He takes a step
He fears his foot will trip on the electrical cord
He shuts his eyes and takes another step
He looks in the vial and sees a rabid pit bull
Will he set the time bomb down fast enough
He lowers the vial
Slowly onto the countertop
He's not careful enough
It spills
Now the doctor is going to die

124

She is midnight

She is the wild side

She screams

She's violent

She's calm

She is silent

131

Marching down the highway
Another secret load
Do you think it will make us sick?
Do you think it will explode?
A lot of flashing lights on top of Humvees
And there's a helicopter flying around
Can you hear the propeller?
My music is drowning out the sound

2

Locked in a war of wills
I'll take the best that you can throw
You'll never break me
Cause I do it for the thrills
And you're a formidable foe
In the end I'll be free
Now I play the cool hand
Predecessor of the one before
You'll never break me
Mister Paul Newman was the man
He was the one to open the door
I am the king of all that I see
You get a battle here and there
Guess who'll be the big winner
You ain't going to break me
Feel like I'm taking a dare
From just a small time sinner
It's never too late to flee
Some say war is hell
But I enjoy a good fight
You will never break me
All's well that ends well
I just know that I'm right
That's the way it will be

124

The clouds hovered in and out of the peaks and crevices of the mountains. Occasionally, they would spit snowflakes at us, but it was April so we knew that they would melt as soon as they hit the limestone and we weren't intimidated. Still, there was that feeling in my gut as if I'd just swallowed one of the millions of yucca plants that tidal waved around us.

I didn't even realize that they were there. Not the yuccas, nor the cactus. Not the rattlesnakes that lounge in the sun on the little shale cliff sides. Not the antelope that you could barely see prancing in the dusk shadows of the foothills. I couldn't see any of that, just the house.

That house.

The garage doors were a blue plastic tarp blowing in an ominous wind. Black particle board enmeshed with chicken wire begging for someone to stucco it, or side it, or waiting for the good Lord himself to hide its own insane nakedness.

Through the slits of my old shutters I could see them occasionally. They'd peek out from behind the blue plastic tarp, or I'd see those stone faces looking out the distorting old windows. I knew that they could see me. A hole had been cut in the particle board so that a video camera could be installed.

The inside of the house, I saw only in my visions.

137

They were
Playing
Frisbee
In their suits
One tie was loosened
One wasn't
But
They were just passing
Time
No
They weren't
Doing anything
Not
One
Damn
Thing

117

Limestone cliffs hued in pink

The sunset mirrors off the lake

Down on the ledge below me is an

Apparently contented rattlesnake

My Dad used to drive me here as a kid

Later, it became the place to go smoke a joint

I can't remember ever having innocence

If I did, Katie helped me lose it at Liberty Point

I doubt that you had been conceived

The first time I looked over this view

I wish I was eighteen and we were in the backseat

But shit, my daughters only a few years younger than you

What's in a name? Why call it Liberty Point?

This is Pueblo, so none of that patriotic bullshit

133

If you wanna deal With me
Be willing
And fucking able To step into the Twilight Zone

Let Rod Serling
Blow a little
Smoke
IN
YOUR FACE

Good Lord
Help
Me
Deal
With a place
That has already
Been
Copyrighted

118

Look at those skinny cables

That's all that's holding it up

My cable is fraying

And they won't hold I know they won't hold

That's all I'm saying

43

Listen to
Water boil
The fury
Scalding chaos
No food
Just rage
True love

6

What a twisted road we've taken
Must have rolled the car at the fork in the road
It was hard to see with the headlights
Staring straight at my face
Felt the gas tank just explode
Air born for a little while
Just another crash and burn

49

Is it wrong to
Waste this paper
On such mundane writing
I pretend its art
And I have something
To say
A drunk on a barstool
Trying to convey
A demented euphoria
Leaking out in the ink

125

Even if you go to hell
And are sentenced to
Eternal damnation
Sooner or later
You're going to
Get used to it
And before you
Know it
The afterlife is going
To be just as
Monotonous
As the present
World is
Oh
Now I get it
I guess you're right

I'm where my
Reservations are
Can I get a
Valet
To park my car

MEMORIAL DAY

Memorial Day
Reminding me of
The old bastard
Across the avenue
Raising the flag
To honor ignorance
And pledge to
Be a hostage of deception
Coming in the name
Of people for people

PSYCHO

It is impossible to prepare
For a meeting with a psycho
You can't truly understand
The evil that crisscrosses
That sick and twisted mind
Of his or hers
Their inborn and instinctual
Lust for chaos and insanity
Is virtually indefensible

129

Having a woman
Is like catching a fish

Some are too small

Some are too big

Some you throw back

Some you keep

But

All of them you eat

DROPS

I love
A woman in
The rain
It washes away her vanity
So that only the
Beauty
Is left there
To
See

121

This world sucks

But I won't back down from it

Maybe

Or at least I don't plan on it

I hope

But I keep a loaded double

barrel shogun

Just in case

135

Hard as it is for me to say
It's fear that's holding me down
There's no way to live without it
Just let me hide inside these walls
Keeping the demons at bay
I pray to God above
Asking for help in some little way
Listening to Aerosmith's "Amazing"
Wishing I could see the light
Still I smoke the resin
But that's two beers a hit
I fucked up again

That's why none of this shit
Makes any sense

THE MILL

The car door shut once
The echo was infinite

The old mill doesn't move anymore
 Men don't come here to work
Sellers don't come to sell
Buyers don't come here to buy

They made some famous steel here
The tanks in world war two
l-beams for the Union Station
Millions of miles of railroad track

Now there is emptiness and ghosts
A lone set of footsteps can be heard
They'll only be audible until I leave
Then silence will be the only sound

As a I remember the fire in the sky
And the pillows of smoke in the day

Whistles blew around the clock
All the taverns sang happy songs
Times were good
Then my childhood went wrong

The markets dried up and layoffs came
A thousand here and a thousand there
The union screamed unfair
But nothing could revive the dying giant

The town almost died too
It isn't that healthy even today
Somehow people keep living
For some strange reason they stay

Two years ago, driving by the mill
You could see a light in the guard's office
That was extinguished as well
There wasn't anything worth guarding

The mill is in my rearview mirror
A place it's been many times before
I always say it's a graveyard
I don't want to go there anymore

www.ingramcontent.com/pod-product-compliance
Lightning Source LLC
Chambersburg PA
CBHW060717030426
42337CB00017B/2904